HOME
SPUN WORDS

PASTOR NELLIE ROBERTS

This book, *Home Spun Words,* is a collection of Pastor Nellie's personal sermon notes and reflections. It contains her words of wisdom, faith and inspiration, captured over the years. These pages offer a glimpse into her heart and the deep spiritual insights she shared with those she led.

HOME SPUN WORDS

ISBN 978-1-0370-5131-9

Printed and bound in South Africa by PRINT ON DEMAND

My Story

All our beginnings are shaped at home, and our lives are spun together by memories with our parents and siblings. My father was an alcoholic, but he got wonderfully born again and began serving the Lord. Neither he nor my mother were hypocrites. Even when he was old and on pension, my father, Bill Ladson, would go out every day handing out flyers and telling people about Jesus. He would go down to the beachfront and put them in the post boxes of all the apartments, always sharing the Good News, and that's the environment I grew up in.

I'll never forget the first miracle I experienced. We were pastoring a church in Estcourt and had come to Durban to visit my mom and dad. We went to the beach, and my daughter Linda, who was about five years old, was playing in the water while I sat beside her. The other children were eating ice cream, and she said, "Ah, Mom, can I have an ice cream?" I said, "My sweetheart, Mommy doesn't have money for ice cream." She replied, "Okay, but let's just ask Jesus anyway."

When I used to pray and cry in my room, she would lie in bed next to me and wipe my tears. She had watched me seek God in prayer so many times that, to her, asking Jesus for a miracle was the natural thing to do. That's why, when I said, "Mommy doesn't have money for ice cream," she simply replied, "Okay, but let's just ask Jesus anyway."

She said, "Let's pray," and so we did. As we sat there in the water, floating toward us on a little wave was a 10-shilling note (about R10). As it reached us, I said, "Look! Jesus has given us enough money to buy an ice cream." That was the first miracle I ever personally witnessed.

As the years went by, I knew I was born again, but I didn't have a real relationship with the Lord. As a preacher's wife, I tried my best, but I felt empty, like a hypocrite, and I was ready to give up.

One Saturday night, while Pastor Fred was in his study praying and preparing for Sunday morning, the devil came knocking at my door, and I decided I was leaving. I had reached my limit. I told Fred, "I'm packing my bags. I'm done. Your Jesus works for you, but He doesn't work for me."

Only God knows where I thought I was going in the middle of the night, but I was serious. I started packing while Fred continued praying in the other room. When he realised what I was doing, he came and stood at the front door, calm but firm. He didn't argue or raise his voice, he just looked at me and said, "Honey, do you see me? Over my dead body are you walking out that door." I snapped back, "Dead body or not, I'm leaving. You can raise the children, you're such a good Christian. I'm done. I'm not getting anywhere." But he didn't let me go.

Earlier that day, someone had given us a cassette tape while we were visiting. It was a message by Kenneth Hagin Sr., an American preacher known for teaching on the importance of faith. I had originally thought, "Fred will enjoy this," but after he wouldn't let me leave, I decided to listen to it myself.

Kenneth Hagin Sr. began to talk about "now faith." It was like a light shone into my heart, my mind and my spirit. Suddenly, I, Nellie Roberts, realised I could ask God right now and He would do it. Until that moment, I had always thought only the Oral Roberts' of the world could ask God and be heard.

We used to sing that song, "Jesus Is Passing This Way," and I would think, "Okay, He didn't touch me this Sunday, maybe next Sunday He'll come by and I'll be lucky." But that night, something changed. The Holy Spirit opened my eyes to Hebrews 11:1: *"Now faith is the substance of things hoped for, the evidence of things not seen."* And when I read that, I started shouting! Fred thought his wife had gone crazy. I yelled, "You have to hear this tape, God is speaking to us!"

That day, something shifted in my spirit. I understood that I, Nellie Roberts, if I believed, God could change things!

In my early years as a preacher's wife, I cleaned toilets, made sure the church was tidy, wore a hat and a long dress and stayed quiet, which was expected of us. One day, I said to Pastor Fred, "What can women actually do in the church? Are we just here to serve you guys like maids?" And he gently said, "No, my sweetheart." You know, Fred, he was always so kind, and he said, "You know the Bible says wives must submit…" I shouted, "SUBMIT?! But the Bible also says that men must love their wives as they love themselves, and you know how much men love themselves!"

Anyway, God opened His Word to me and I devoured the New Testament from Matthew to Revelation. I read it over and over again. It was life to me, absolute life. Our marriage wasn't good at the time. I felt like I was failing my children, like I wasn't a good mother. All those thoughts the devil plants in your mind. But then I read Psalm 139, where God said, "Even before you were born, I knew you. I created you, and I have plans for you."

Me? God has plans for me?

I was struggling emotionally and mentally, and Pastor Fred said, "Let's go to America." People had been calling him to preach at their churches, and our son Llewellyn, daughter Wendy, and son-in-law Neville were all there at "Christ for the Nations" Bible school.

So we went to America. Pastor Fred had many speaking engagements, and one day while cleaning the house, I opened my Bible and read: "Love others as you love yourself." I cried out, "Lord, how can I love others when inside I'm filled with criticism and ugliness? I don't say kind things to people, I feel like a police-man!"

As I poured out my heart to God, I saw an image appear, as if on a screen, like a TV. A rose appeared, my favourite flower and the Holy Spirit asked, "Would you ever say to this rose, 'I hate you'?" I said, "Never, Lord, because You created it." And He said, "I created you."

Then He asked, "How do you want Me to forgive you?" I remembered 1 John 1:9: *"If we confess our sins, He is faithful and just to forgive us and cleanse us from all unrighteousness."* He said, "If you want Me to, I will cleanse you right now and never hold it against you again." And I asked, "Never again?" He said, "Never again."

I cried and asked, "Lord, why do I think like this? Since I was a little girl, I've always felt like I wasn't good enough." And the Lord reminded me: "When you were a child, you ran to your daddy to be picked up and loved, but he didn't realise that. He pushed you aside. From that moment, the devil planted a lie in your mind that you shouldn't be here."

Then I saw another rose, but tiny insects were eating the base of it. I said, "Shame, Lord, the insects are destroying the rose." And He said, "That's what unforgiveness, criticism and bitterness do when you allow them in your life. But I'll forgive you."

I began confessing every sin I could remember, even secrets no one else knew. My stomach began to shake (which is impossible to do in the natural) and I ran to the bathroom. As I began to heave, the Lord spoke: "There goes fear."

The spirit of fear, doubt and unbelief left me that day. It's not about how long you pray or how good you've been. The Lord just wants your heart, your mind and your love. Pastor Fred used to say, "Long prayers in public mean short prayers at home, but short prayers in public mean long prayers at home."

After that experience, I changed. I used to criticise Fred's sermons and say, "That was terrible! I don't know how the people listened." I was ugly because I was hurting. Often, people who lash out do so because they feel rejected, it's a spirit.

But after that breakthrough in our lounge, I became joyful. I was so excited about what Jesus had done, and I had never been so happy. When Fred would come home, I'd say, "That was the best sermon you've ever preached! You're the best husband! These other guys can go sleep, you're the best!" After a month, he sat me down and asked, "I love what you're doing, but I can't get used to this woman that you've become. Are you sure you haven't been drinking? I've never seen you this happy."

The truth is, God made us, but none of us is perfect. He's working on all of us. That's why we can't point fingers at others. It's easy to look at someone in church and say, "Look at that deacon, he's a demon!" But we all need help. The Word is supposed to heal us, not puff us up.

Many people struggle in marriage because of emotional wounds or traumatic sexual experiences in their youth. But Jesus was there when it happened. He understands. He hears you when you cry. He understands your pain. If you want God to heal you, you need to be truthful and honest. Don't play games with God; you either trust Him completely or you don't.

Your husband might be broken, too. Men don't talk like we do, us girls, we've got big mouths! But men keep everything inside. The Bible says in Ephesians, *"Husbands, love your wives,"* and *"Wives, respect and encourage your husbands."*

Say things like, "Thank you for your hard work. Thank you for looking after us and for this home. Thank you for being a good husband." Those simple words, spoken sincerely, can transform a marriage. They can change you and even change your children. We all want our kids to come to Jesus, but they watch what we do more than what we say. They don't care how loud you preach; it's about how you live at home.

In 1979, God called us back to South Africa from America with the mandate to open a church, A House of Prayer for All Nations. We obeyed Him, and Durban Christian Centre was established. Pastor Fred was already 60 years old at the time, and we received a word of prophecy to build.

We became the first church in South Africa to establish a non-racial, non-political congregation. We absolutely refused to be a political church. One day, while I was praying, the Lord told me to write something down. He said, "It's My church. It's My people. It's My money." I thought, "Yes, it's Jesus' church." And I remembered the promise in Matthew 16:18: "I will build My church, and the gates of Hades shall not prevail against it." So yes, we were building a building, but really, we were building people for the Kingdom of God.

It was never our church. It wasn't Fred Roberts' church either. When you close your eyes and step into the presence of God, you take nothing with you, not even your body. Nothing belongs to us. When we stand before the Lord in Heaven, He won't say, "Welcome, Big Chief Apostle" or give us any grand title. He'll simply say, "Well done, good and faithful servant." That's why we should all call ourselves servants. Forget about trying to be an Apostle for the title, your "Apostle story" is about doing the work: getting souls saved, working hard and not sitting around with too much time on your hands.

Some people think ministry means no work, but the truth is, there are souls to be saved. Jesus said, "My church, My people,

My money." It's His church, His people, and His money. And if it's Jesus' money, it doesn't belong to us. That's what we learned.

When we started building, we had no money. Pastor Fred never had money, but God would give him a dream. He would stand before the congregation and say, "Folks, the Lord said to me this is what we must do." That was all he needed to say, because people trusted him with Jesus' money.

One day, we were at a shopping mall when a gentleman came up, shook Pastor Fred's hand and said something I'll never forget. He said, "You know, Pastor Fred, yours is the only church in Durban where we can give our money and trust it will be used right." And he was a wealthy man, which made this a true compliment.

Someone once asked Pastor Fred, "What is the sign of a true Apostle?" He answered, "Humility." Another time, a group of preachers asked him, "What's the greatest compliment you've ever received?" And he said, "When a little child hears me preach and runs up and says, 'I gave my heart to Jesus.'" That, to him, was the highest honour.

So it's not about us. It's not what we do in ourselves. We do what we do because we love Him.

Fred and I were married for 64 years and had a wonderful marriage. When the time came to say goodbye to my husband, it was our wedding anniversary. He knew he was going into eternity. I was kissing him, loving him and thanking him for being such a wonderful husband. And he looked at me and said, "Sweetheart, they've made a big mistake today." I asked, "What mistake?" and he said, "They're going to have a party for us at the Jesus Dome, the church, but I'm going home to be with Jesus." Tears started streaming down his face. He said, "Instead of celebrating our anniversary, they should be celebrating my graduation to heaven. I'm going home to be with Jesus."

I once had an experience of going up to Heaven. I found myself sitting in a beautiful park on a chair, listening to the most incredible orchestra. I mean, you've never heard music like this; it was absolutely beautiful. As I was listening, I looked down and noticed someone sitting next to me. I saw scars from nails in His feet. I tried to look up to see who it was, and He took my hand. When I looked at His wrist, I saw the hole. And then I came back.

That's why I am so committed to worship. I don't understand all these modern songs that people sing about themselves. I only know true worship, and it's about Him. There is a sound in Heaven, and once you've heard that sound, nothing on earth compares to it.

It was a deeply difficult time when the doctors told us that Pastor Fred had a serious lung-degenerating condition. I had so many questions. He never smoked. He never drank. He was full of faith right to the end, always speaking and believing the Word. I kept asking God, "Why him?"

One morning, we were sitting together having coffee. He was too weak to get out of bed, and each morning we would pray and take communion together. That morning, something extraordinary happened. While we were sitting together through the open sliding door, a little dove flew right into our bedroom, landed on his bed, walked around a few times, then hopped onto his bedside table and flew out. We never saw it again.

Still, I kept asking, "Why, Lord?"

Then one morning when I woke up, I don't know if it was a dream or a vision, but in my bedroom, where we had our two prayer chairs, I saw Jesus sitting in my chair. He was laughing! He threw His head back with the most joyful laugh. I stood there with my hand over my mouth and said, "Jesus, I don't know why

You're laughing like that!" But He kept laughing with such joy. Then He said, "The joy of the Lord is your strength, Nellie."

You know, the spiritual realm isn't something you can fully explain. It wasn't spooky or strange; it felt so natural, like you and I having a conversation. That's how precious Jesus is.

This is a short version of some of my experiences with the Lord. In our book All Things Are Possible, we share much more.

I married a wonderful man. God gave us four beautiful children, and believe me, I prayed hard for them! Some of them were very naughty at times, but today, they're all serving the Lord. I can truly say, like David, *"I have been young and now I'm old, but I have never seen the righteous forsaken, nor their children begging for bread"* (Psalm 37:25 NKJV). We now have grandchildren and great-grandchildren, and I know they will all serve the Lord, too. I can honestly say, I've been so privileged and abundantly blessed by the Lord.

And if God can take someone like me and use them, He can do it for anyone who believes that with God, all things are possible.

"Long prayers in public mean short prayers at home. Short prayers in public mean long prayers at home."

Dr Fred Roberts

Dr Fred Roberts graduated to Heaven on 13 November 2017

&

Pastor Nellie Roberts graduated to Heaven on 29 June 2024

CONTENTS

Chapter 1

The Call to Possess the Land

God has called us to walk in victory, in our spirit, soul and body, but we must actively possess the promises He has given us.

Just as Israel had to enter and take the land that God had promised them, we too must step into the fullness of what He has prepared for us. The call to possess the land is not just a historical account; it is a spiritual principle that applies to every believer today.

God has already prepared blessings, breakthroughs and supernatural favour for us as His children, but He requires our participation. Just as the Israelites had to cross the Jordan, march around Jericho and fight for their inheritance, we must step out in faith, obey His Word and claim what is rightfully ours in Christ.

God's Command to Joshua

Joshua 1:1–9 (NKJV)

"After the death of Moses the servant of the Lord, it came to pass that the Lord spoke to Joshua the son of Nun, Moses' assistant, saying: 'Moses My servant is dead. Now therefore, arise, go over this Jordan, you and all this people, to the land which I am giving to them – the children of Israel. Every place that the sole of your foot will tread upon I have given you, as I said to Moses... Have I not commanded you? Be strong and of good courage; do not be afraid, nor be dismayed, for the Lord your God is with you wherever you go.'"

God's call to Joshua was a call to take action. Though the land was promised, it would not be handed over without a fight. The same applies to us today; God's promises are real and available, but they must be pursued and possessed by faith.

What Does It Mean to Possess the Land?

1. **Recognising What's Already Yours** – We must realise that through Christ, we already have victory, healing, provision and peace. Ephesians 1:3 tells us that we have been blessed with every spiritual blessing in Christ. The challenge is not if God will give, it's whether we will step into what He has already provided.

2. **Walking in Obedience** – Possession requires obedience to God's direction. When God told the Israelites to march around Jericho, their victory was tied to their obedience, not their logic.
   When He calls us to take action, whether in our careers, ministries, or personal lives, our willingness to obey positions us to receive His best.

3. **Overcoming Fear with Faith** – God repeatedly told Joshua, "Be strong and courageous." Fear is the enemy of possession! Many times, we hesitate to step into God's promises because of doubt, fear of failure, or fear of the unknown. But faith activates the supernatural.

Genesis 1:28 (NKJV)

"Then God blessed them, and God said to them, 'Be fruitful and multiply; fill the earth and subdue it; have dominion over the fish of the sea, over the birds of the air, and over every living thing that moves on the earth.'"

From the very beginning, God's plan was for mankind to walk in dominion. We were created not to be victims of circumstances, but to rule and reign through faith in Christ.

Keys to Possessing the Promises of God

- **Align Your Thoughts with God's Word** – Renew your mind with the truth of Scripture (Romans 12:2).
- **Declare What God Has Said** – Speak His promises over your life (Proverbs 18:21).
- **Take Faith Steps** – Faith requires action; be willing to move forward (James 2:17).
- **Stay in Position** – Many people miss their blessing because they step out of God's timing. Be patient and steadfast (Galatians 6:9).

Obstacles to Possessing the Land

The Israelites faced giants, walls and fierce opposition before stepping into their promised land. Likewise, we face obstacles that can hinder us from receiving what God has promised us.

- **Doubt and Unbelief** – If we question God's ability, we limit His power in our lives.
- **Fear of Change** – Many people stay in bondage because the unknown feels scarier than their current situation.
- **Disobedience** – The Israelites who doubted and disobeyed wandered in the wilderness for 40 years. Delayed obedience is still disobedience.

Possessing the Land Requires Boldness

To possess what God has for you, you must be bold. It requires a shift from a survival mindset to a victory mindset. Joshua and Caleb saw the giants, but they believed God's power was greater. We, too, must be willing to see beyond the natural and trust in the supernatural ability of God.

Numbers 13:30 (NKJV)

"Then Caleb quieted the people before Moses, and said, 'Let us go up at once and take possession, for we are well able to overcome it.'"

HOME SPUN WORD

- God has already given you His promises, but you must claim them by faith.

- Don't sit back waiting for blessings to fall into your lap; step into them!

- Fear will try to stop you, but courage in God will move you forward.

- Courage is not the absence of fear; it is moving forward despite fear.

- Walking in obedience is the key to possessing all God has for you.

- Just as Joshua obeyed God's instructions, so must we.

What promises has God spoken over your life? What dreams has He placed in your heart? The time to step forward is now! Just as God told Joshua to arise and go, He is calling you to move in faith today.

"Don't feel guilty about your adult children's choices, you are not responsible."

Pastor Nellie Roberts

Chapter 2

The Battlefield of the Mind

The greatest battle we will ever fight is not against external circumstances; it is in our minds. The enemy knows that if he can control our thoughts, he can control our lives.

This is why the Bible tells us to renew our minds and take every thought captive to the obedience of Christ.

Our thoughts shape our actions, our attitudes and ultimately, our destiny. If we don't guard our minds, we will be filled with doubt, fear and insecurity, unable to walk in the fullness of God's promises.

Winning the Battle in Your Mind

Mark 12:30 (NKJV)

"And you shall love the Lord your God with all your heart, with all your soul, with all your mind, and with all your strength. This is the first commandment."

Romans 12:1–2 (NKJV)

"I beseech you therefore, brethren, by the mercies of God, that you present your bodies a living sacrifice, holy, acceptable to God, which is your reasonable service. And do not be conformed to this world, but be transformed by the renewing of your mind, that you may prove what is that good and acceptable and perfect will of God."

Three Types of Minds That Keep Us from Victory

1. **The Carnal Mind** – A mind dominated by the flesh and worldly thinking. It resists the things of God.
   o Romans 8:7 (NKJV)
     "Because the carnal mind is enmity against God; for it is not subject to the law of God, nor indeed can be."

2. **The Passive Mind** – A mind that doesn't actively resist negative thoughts. It allows anything to take root.
   o Proverbs 4:23 (NKJV)
     "Keep your heart with all diligence, for out of it spring the issues of life."
3. **The Oppressed Mind** – A mind weighed down by the enemy's lies, leading to fear, anxiety and depression.
   o 2 Timothy 1:7 (NKJV)
     "For God has not given us a spirit of fear, but of power and of love and of a sound mind."

The Renewed Mind in Christ

A renewed mind, transformed by God's Word, is a mind that walks in faith, peace and victory. It recognises the lies of the enemy and replaces them with the truth of God's word.

James 3:15–17 (NKJV)
"This wisdom does not descend from above, but is earthly, sensual, demonic. For where envy and self-seeking exist, confusion and every evil thing are there. But the wisdom that is from above is first pure, then peaceable, gentle, willing to yield, full of mercy and good fruits, without partiality and without hypocrisy."

How to Renew Your Mind Daily

1. **Meditate on God's Word** – Fill your mind with Scripture and allow it to shape your thoughts.
   o Joshua 1:8 (NKJV)
     "This Book of the Law shall not depart from your mouth, but you shall meditate in it day and night, that you may observe to do according to all that is written in it. For then you will make your way prosperous, and then you will have good success."

2. **Guard Your Thought Life** – Be intentional about what you allow into your mind.
   o Philippians 4:8 (NKJV)
   "Finally, brethren, whatever things are true, whatever things are noble, whatever things are just, whatever things are pure, whatever things are lovely, whatever things are of good report, if there is any virtue and if there is anything praiseworthy – meditate on these things."

3. **Take Every Thought Captive** – Reject every thought that is contrary to God's Word and renew your mind with His truth.
   o 2 Corinthians 10:4–5 (NKJV)
   "For the weapons of our warfare are not carnal but mighty in God for pulling down strongholds, casting down arguments and every high thing that exalts itself against the knowledge of God, bringing every thought into captivity to the obedience of Christ."

4. **Speak Life Over Your Mind** – Your words have the power to shape your thoughts, attitudes and your reality.
   o Proverbs 18:21 (NKJV)
   "Death and life are in the power of the tongue, and those who love it will eat its fruit."

5. **Surround Yourself with Faith-Building People** – Your environment matters; it influences your thinking.
   o Hebrews 10:25 (NKJV)
   "Not forsaking the assembling of ourselves together, as is the manner of some, but exhorting one another, and so much the more as you see the Day approaching."

The Power of a Renewed Mind

When your mind is renewed by God's Word, you walk in peace. You're no longer controlled by emotions, circumstances, or the opinions of others, but by the truth of God.

Isaiah 26:3 (NKJV)
"You will keep him in perfect peace, whose mind is stayed on You, because he trusts in You."

Biblical Examples of a Renewed Mind

- **David defeating Goliath** – While others saw a giant, David saw an opportunity for God's power to be displayed (1 Samuel 17:45–47).
- **Jesus in the wilderness** – Jesus resisted the enemy by declaring the Word of God (Matthew 4:1–11).
- **Paul in prison** – Despite being in chains, Paul's mind was fixed on Christ and he encouraged others with joy and contentment (Philippians 4:11–13).

HOME SPUN WORD

- Your mind determines your victory or your defeat.

- Renew your mind daily with God's Word.

- Take captive every thought that contradicts God's truth.

- Speak life and stay connected to faith-filled people.

Are you struggling with fear, doubt, or negative thinking? Start today by renewing your mind through the Word of God. Commit to filling your thoughts with His promises and watch how your life transforms as you begin to walk in the victory of a renewed mind.

Taking Responsibility for Your Choices

God has given us free will, and the choices we make shape our lives.

Too often, people blame their circumstances on others when in reality, it's our own decisions that determine our destiny. Every day, we face choices, some small and some life-changing, but all of them influence the path we walk by faith.

Taking responsibility for your choices is a sign of spiritual maturity. It means recognising that your actions, thoughts and responses shape your future. Instead of waiting for someone else to change your situation, you must take ownership and walk in obedience to God's direction.

God's First Command of Responsibility

Genesis 2:16–17 (NKJV)

"And the Lord God commanded the man, saying, 'Of every tree of the garden you may freely eat; but of the tree of the knowledge of good and evil you shall not eat, for in the day that you eat of it you shall surely die.'"

God placed Adam and Eve in the Garden with clear instructions and everything they needed. But He still gave them a choice, to obey or disobey. Their decision to eat from the Tree of Knowledge introduced sin into the world, showing us the powerful consequences of a single choice.

Even today, God presents us with the same principle: we must choose to obey His word, walk in faith and take responsibility for our own lives.

The Power of Choice - YES and NO are the two most powerful words you can say!

Deuteronomy 30:19 (NKJV) declares:

"I call Heaven and earth as witnesses today against you, that I have set before you life and death, blessing and cursing; therefore choose life, that both you and your descendants may live."

God gives us the power to choose, but He also warns us that our choices come with consequences. Our decisions determine whether we walk in blessing or struggle in disobedience.

Common Obstacles to Taking Responsibility

Many people struggle with taking responsibility because of certain emotional and spiritual barriers:

- **Blame-Shifting** – Just like Adam and Eve, we often blame others instead of taking responsibility for our own choices.
  - Genesis 3:12–13 (NKJV)
    "The woman whom You gave to be with me, she gave me of the tree, and I ate...
    The serpent deceived me, and I ate."

- **Fear of Failure** – Some people avoid responsibility because they're afraid of making the wrong choice.
  - Joshua 1:9 (NKJV)
    "Be strong and of good courage; do not be afraid...
    for the Lord your God is with you wherever you go."

- **Pride and Stubbornness** – It takes humility to admit we're wrong.
  - Proverbs 16:18 (NKJV)
    "Pride goes before destruction, and a haughty spirit before a fall."

- **Victim Mentality** – Believing life is just "happening to us" keeps us powerless; we have the power to choose.
  - Romans 8:37 (NKJV)
    "Yet in all these things we are more than conquerors through Him who loved us."

- **Lack of Knowledge** – Without understanding God's Word, people live passively.
  - Hosea 4:6 (NKJV)
    "My people are destroyed for lack of knowledge."

- **Procrastination and Laziness** – Delaying decisions leads to stagnation.
  - Proverbs 13:4 (NKJV)
    "The soul of a lazy man desires, and has nothing; but the soul of the diligent shall be made rich."

- **Emotional Immaturity** – Reacting emotionally instead of responding with wisdom.
  - Proverbs 14:29 (NKJV)
    "He who is slow to wrath has great understanding, but he who is impulsive exalts folly."

- **Influence of Others** – Wrong associations can pull us off course.
  - 1 Corinthians 15:33 (NKJV)
    "Do not be deceived: 'Evil company corrupts good habits.'"

- **Spiritual Warfare** – The enemy works to keep us trapped in blame, fear and passivity.
  - 2 Corinthians 10:4–5 (NKJV)
    *"The weapons of our warfare are not carnal but mighty in God
    for pulling down strongholds... bringing every thought into captivity to the obedience of Christ."*

- **Lack of Trust in God** – Some resist responsibility because they don't fully trust that God will guide them through the consequences of their decisions.

- Proverbs 3:5–6 (NKJV)
  "Trust in the Lord with all your heart, and lean not on your own understanding;
  In all your ways acknowledge Him, and He shall direct your paths."

Our Three Key Areas of Responsibility

- **Spiritual Responsibility** – Seeking God daily and growing in your faith.
- **Emotional Responsibility** – Guarding your hearts and thoughts (Proverbs 4:23).
- **Practical Responsibility** – Managing your time, finances and relationships wisely.

How to Take Responsibility for Your Choices

- **Acknowledge Your Role** – Stop blaming others and take ownership of your actions.
- **Seek Wisdom Through Prayer** – Ask God to guide your decision-making (James 1:5).
- **Take Faith Steps** – Faith requires action; do not be passive, move in faith.
- **Accept Correction and Learn from Mistakes** – Real growth happens when we learn from our mistakes and make the necessary changes.
- **Surround Yourself with Godly Counsel** – Find wise mentors who keep you accountable and on track.

Biblical Examples of Responsibility

- **The Prodigal Son** (Luke 15:11–24) – He made poor choices, but he took responsibility, repented and returned to his father.
- **King David** (Psalm 51) – After his sin with Bathsheba, David repented and took ownership of his failure.

- **Daniel** (Daniel 6:10–23) – He remained faithful in prayer despite the king's decree and took responsibility for his faith.

HOME SPUN WORD

- Your life is shaped by the choices you make.

- God has given you the power to choose wisely.

- Responsibility leads to maturity, and maturity brings blessing.

God is calling you to step into your divine destiny by taking responsibility for your thoughts, words and actions. Today is the day to stop making excuses and start walking in faith, obedience and wisdom. When you do, you will see the hand of God move powerfully in your life.

Chapter 4

Walking in the Authority of Christ

One of the greatest truths we must grasp as believers is that we have been given authority through Christ. Many Christians live defeated lives because they do not understand or exercise the authority God has given them. But when we walk in our God-given authority, we rise above fear, oppression and the enemy's attacks. Jesus did not come only to save us; He came to restore the authority that was lost in the Garden of Eden. Through Him, we have the power to overcome every work of darkness, walk in victory and establish His Kingdom on earth.

We Have Authority Given by Christ

Luke 10:19 (NKJV)
"Behold, I give you the authority to trample on serpents and scorpions, and over all the power of the enemy, and nothing shall by any means hurt you."

Jesus has given us authority, not just to survive, but to thrive and triumph over the enemy. However, if we do not understand this authority, we will fail to exercise it and live far beneath our potential in Christ.

Understanding Your Authority in Christ

- **Authority Over the Enemy** – Satan no longer has dominion over those who are in Christ. Jesus stripped him of his power at the cross.
  - Colossians 2:15 (NKJV)
    "Having disarmed principalities and powers, He made a public spectacle of them, triumphing over them in it."
- **Authority Through the Word** – The power of the spoken Word of God is a weapon against darkness.

- Matthew 4:4 (NKJV)
  "But He answered and said, 'It is written, 'Man shall not live by bread alone, but by every word that proceeds from the mouth of God.'"

- **Authority in Prayer** – We have been given the power to pray and see results.
  - John 14:13–14 (NKJV)
    "And whatever you ask in My name, that I will do, that the Father may be glorified in the Son. If you ask anything in My name, I will do it."

How to Walk in Spiritual Authority

- **Know Your Identity in Christ** – Authority comes from knowing who you are as a child of God.
  - Romans 8:17 (NKJV)
    "And if children, then heirs – heirs of God and joint heirs with Christ, if indeed we suffer with Him, that we may also be glorified together."

- **Speak and Declare God's Word** – The power of life and death is in the tongue.
  - Proverbs 18:21 (NKJV)
    "Death and life are in the power of the tongue, and those who love it will eat its fruit."

- **Resist the Devil** – When you stand firm in faith, the enemy must flee.
  - James 4:7 (NKJV)
    "Therefore submit to God. Resist the devil and he will flee from you."

- **Live in Righteousness (Live Right)** – Sin weakens spiritual authority, but righteousness strengthens it.

o Proverbs 28:1 (NKJV)
"The wicked flee when no one pursues, but the righteous are bold as a lion."

Biblical Examples of Walking in Authority

- **Jesus Casting Out Demons** – Jesus demonstrated the authority believers should walk in.
  - o Mark 1:27 (NKJV)
    "Then they were all amazed, so that they questioned among themselves, saying, 'What is this? What new doctrine is this? For with authority He commands even the unclean spirits, and they obey Him.'"

- **Peter and John Healing the Lame Man** – They exercised their authority in the name of Jesus.
  - o Acts 3:6 (NKJV)
    "Then Peter said, 'Silver and gold I do not have, but what I do have I give you: In the name of Jesus Christ of Nazareth, rise up and walk.'"

- **Paul Casting Out a Spirit of Divination** – Paul knew his authority and used it to silence the enemy.
  - o Acts 16:18 (NKJV)
    "And this she did for many days. But Paul, greatly annoyed, turned and said to the spirit, 'I command you in the name of Jesus Christ to come out of her.' And he came out that very hour."

Take Dominion Over Your Life

Many believers tolerate things they have the authority to change. Jesus did not die for us to live in fear, oppression, bondage, depression or rejection. He gave us the power to speak, declare and command victory in our lives.

- **Take Authority Over Fear** – Fear is a tool of the enemy, but perfect love casts it out.
  - ○ 2 Timothy 1:7 (NKJV)
    "For God has not given us a spirit of fear, but of power and of love and of a sound mind."

- **Command Sickness to Leave** – Jesus bore our sickness on the cross, and we have the right to claim healing. There is power in the blood of Jesus.
  - ○ Isaiah 53:5 (NKJV)
    "But He was wounded for our transgressions, He was bruised for our iniquities; the chastisement for our peace was upon Him, and by His stripes we are healed."

- **Declare Financial Provision** – God is our provider, and He desires for His children to walk in abundance.
  - ○ Philippians 4:19 (NKJV)
    "And my God shall supply all your need according to His riches in glory by Christ Jesus."

HOME SPUN WORD

- Christ has given us authority over every work of darkness.

- Walking in authority requires faith, boldness and righteousness.

- Use prayer, the Word and your spoken confession to enforce victory.

Are you walking in the authority Christ has given you?

It's time to rise up in faith and use the power of God's Word, prayer and obedience to enforce victory in your life. You are not powerless; you are an overcomer in Christ!

Chapter 5

The Power of Faith and Spiritual Warfare

Faith is the key that unlocks the power of God in our lives. Without faith, we cannot fully access the promises of God. Yet walking in faith is not always easy, because we are engaged in a spiritual battle. The enemy fights against our faith, knowing that a faith-filled believer is unstoppable.

The Bible makes it clear that our fight is not against flesh and blood, but against spiritual forces that seek to hinder us from walking in victory. The good news is that God has equipped us with everything we need to overcome.

Faith Is the Foundation of Spiritual Victory

Hebrews 11:1 (NKJV)
"Now faith is the substance of things hoped for, the evidence of things not seen."

Faith is not merely wishful thinking; it is the confident assurance that what God has spoken will come to pass. When we walk in faith, we are declaring that God's Word is the final authority in our lives, regardless of what our circumstances may look like.

The Reality of Spiritual Warfare

Ephesians 6:12 (NKJV)
"For we do not wrestle against flesh and blood, but against principalities, against powers, against the rulers of the darkness of this age, against spiritual hosts of wickedness in the heavenly places."

As believers, we are in a constant battle. The enemy wants to keep us in doubt, fear and defeat, but God has given us the spiritual weapons to stand firm and walk in victory.

How Faith and Spiritual Warfare Work Together

- **Faith Activates the Power of God** – Without faith, we cannot access God's promises (Hebrews 11:6).

- **Spiritual Warfare Requires the Armour of God** – We must put on the full armour to stand against the devil's schemes (Ephesians 6:13–17).

- **Victory Comes Through Persistent Prayer** – Praying in faith brings supernatural breakthroughs (Mark 11:24).

- **Speaking God's Word Is a Weapon** – Jesus overcame Satan by declaring Scripture (Matthew 4:4).

- **Praise and Worship Are Acts of War** – Worship shifts the atmosphere and confuses the enemy (2 Chronicles 20:22).

- **The Armour of God** – Our Spiritual Defence.

  Ephesians 6:13–17 (NKJV)
  "Therefore take up the whole armour of God, that you may be able to withstand in the evil day, and having done all, to stand. Stand therefore, having girded your waist with truth, having put on the breastplate of righteousness, and having shod your feet with the preparation of the gospel of peace; above all, taking the shield of faith with which you will be able to quench all the fiery darts of the wicked one. And take the helmet of salvation, and the sword of the Spirit, which is the word of God."

The Armour of God:

- **The Belt of Truth** – Stand on the truth of God's Word.
- **The Breastplate of Righteousness** – Live a life of holiness and obedience.
- **The Shoes of Peace** – Walk in the peace of God and be ready to share the Gospel.
- **The Shield of Faith** – Defend against doubt and fear.
- **The Helmet of Salvation** – Guard your mind against the lies of the enemy.
- **The Sword of the Spirit (God's Word)** – Declare Scripture to defeat the enemy.

How to Strengthen Your Faith for Battle

- **Feed on God's Word** – Faith comes by hearing and hearing by the Word of God (Romans 10:17).
- **Speak Words of Faith** – Life and death are in the power of the tongue (Proverbs 18:21).
- **Resist Fear and Doubt** – God has not given us a spirit of fear (2 Timothy 1:7).
- **Stay in Prayer and Worship** – These are powerful weapons against the enemy (Psalm 149:6).
- **Surround Yourself with Strong Believers** – Fellowship strengthens our faith (Hebrews 10:25).

Biblical Examples of Faith and Spiritual Warfare

- **David vs. Goliath** – David's faith defeated the giant when others were afraid (1 Samuel 17:45–47).
- **Jesus Overcoming Satan in the Wilderness** – Jesus used the Word of God to resist the enemy (Matthew 4:1–11).
- **Paul and Silas in Prison** – They worshipped despite their circumstances, and God delivered them (Acts 16:25–26).
- **Jehoshaphat's Victory Through Worship** – As they praised, God fought their battle (2 Chronicles 20:21–22).

HOME SPUN WORD

- Faith is essential to possessing God's promises.

- Spiritual warfare is real, but victory belongs to those who stand firm.

- Strengthen your faith through the Word, prayer, worship and confession.

- Use the full armour of God to withstand every attack of the enemy.

Are you facing a battle today?

Strengthen your faith, put on your armour and stand firm in God's promises.
The enemy has already been defeated; now walk in the victory that is yours in Christ!

" *Never borrow money from anyone, have your own stuff.* **"**
Pastor Nellie Roberts

Chapter 6

Perseverance and Endurance in Faith

Faith is not just about believing for a moment; it's about standing firm over time. Many people start strong in faith but grow weary when trials arise. True victory comes through endurance. The promises of God often require persistence, and only those who endure will receive what has been promised.

We Need Perseverance

James 1:2–4 (NKJV)
"My brethren, count it all joy when you fall into various trials,
knowing that the testing of your faith produces patience.
But let patience have its perfect work, that you may be perfect and
complete, lacking nothing."

Life happens, and trials will come, but how we respond to the trials will determine the outcome. Perseverance is the ability to keep going despite difficulties, trusting that God is working all things together for our good.

Why Perseverance Matters

- **Faith Is Tested Through Trials** – Every believer will face tests, but endurance strengthens us.
  - 1 Peter 1:6–7 (NKJV)
    "In this you greatly rejoice, though now for a little while,
    if need be, you have been grieved by various trials, that
    the genuineness of your faith, being much more precious
    than gold that perishes, though it is tested by fire, may
    be found to praise, honour, and glory at the revelation of
    Jesus Christ."
- **Endurance Produces Maturity** – Just as an athlete trains for a marathon, spiritual perseverance builds character.
  - Romans 5:3–4 (NKJV)
    "And not only that, but we also glory in tribulations,
    knowing that tribulation produces perseverance; and
    perseverance, character; and character, hope."

- **Holding Onto God's Promises Brings Reward** – Those who endure will receive what God has promised.
  - o Hebrews 10:36 (NKJV)
    "For you have need of endurance, so that after you have done the will of God, you may receive the promise."

How to Develop Endurance

- **Keep Your Eyes on Jesus** – He is our ultimate example of perseverance.
  - o Hebrews 12:1–2 (NKJV)
    "Let us run with endurance the race that is set before us, looking unto Jesus, the author and finisher of our faith..."
- **Stay Rooted in God's Word** – The Word strengthens us when we feel weak.
  - o Psalm 119:105 (NKJV)
    "Your word is a lamp to my feet and a light to my path."
- **Maintain a Lifestyle of Prayer** – Prayer fuels endurance and faith.
  - o Luke 18:1 (NKJV)
    "Then He spoke a parable to them, that men always ought to pray and not lose heart."
- **Surround Yourself with Faithful Believers** – Encouragement from fellow believers helps us stay strong.
  - o Galatians 6:9–10 (NKJV)
    "And let us not grow weary while doing good, for in due season we shall reap if we do not lose heart."

Biblical Examples of Perseverance

- **Job's Faith in Trials** – Job lost everything but remained faithful, and God restored him (Job 42:10).

- **Paul's Endurance in Ministry** – Despite shipwrecks, beatings and imprisonment, Paul never gave up (2 Corinthians 11:23–27).

- **Abraham Waiting for God's Promise** – Abraham waited years for Isaac, trusting in God's timing (Romans 4:20–21).

HOME SPUN WORD

- Trials refine and strengthen our faith.

- Endurance leads to spiritual maturity and blessings.

- Stay focused on Jesus, remain in the Word and keep pressing forward in faith.

God is not looking for people who start strong and give up when it gets hard; He's looking for those who persevere. The blessing is in the enduring.

Chapter 7
Overcoming Doubt and Standing Firm in Faith

Doubt is one of the biggest obstacles to walking in faith. It sneaks in when we face delays, opposition or uncertainty. However, God calls us to stand firm in faith and resist doubt.

The Danger of Doubt

James 1:6–8 (NKJV)
"But let him ask in faith, with no doubting, for he who doubts is like a wave of the sea driven and tossed by the wind.
For let not that man suppose that he will receive anything from the Lord; he is a double-minded man, unstable in all his ways."

Doubt weakens faith and keeps us from receiving God's best. The enemy uses doubt to hinder our prayers, delay our breakthroughs and keep us from walking in victory.

How Does Doubt Creep In?

- **When We Focus on Circumstances Instead of God's Promises** – Peter began to sink when he took his eyes off Jesus.
  o Matthew 14:30–31 (NKJV)
  "But when he saw that the wind was boisterous, he was afraid; and beginning to sink he cried out, saying, 'Lord, save me!'
  And immediately Jesus stretched out His hand and caught him, and said to him, 'O you of little faith, why did you doubt?'"

- **When We Let Fear Take Control** – Fear and faith cannot operate together.
  o 2 Timothy 1:7 (NKJV)
  "For God has not given us a spirit of fear, but of power and of love and of a sound mind."

- **When We Lack Knowledge of God's Word** – The more we know God's Word, the stronger our faith becomes.

- Hosea 4:6 (NKJV)
  "My people are destroyed for lack of knowledge."

- **When We Listen to the Wrong Voices** – The Israelites fell into doubt because they listened to the ten fearful spies instead of trusting the faith-filled report of Caleb and Joshua.
  - Numbers 13:31–33 (NKJV)
    "But the men who had gone up with him said, 'We are not able to go up against the people, for they are stronger than we.'"

How to Overcome Doubt

- **Feed Your Faith with God's Word**
  - Romans 10:17 (NKJV)
    "Faith comes by hearing, and hearing by the Word of God."

- **Declare God's Promises Boldly**
  - Proverbs 18:21 (NKJV)
    "Death and life are in the power of the tongue."

- **Pray with Expectation**
  - Matthew 21:22 (NKJV)
    "And whatever things you ask in prayer, believing, you will receive."

- **Refuse to Entertain Negative Thoughts**
  - 2 Corinthians 10:5 (NKJV)
    "...bringing every thought into captivity to the obedience of Christ."

- **Trust in God's Character** – Know that He is faithful to fulfil what He has promised.
  - Numbers 23:19 (NKJV)
    "God is not a man, that He should lie, nor a son of man, that He should repent.

Has He said, and will He not do? Or has He spoken, and will He not make it good?"

- **Be Patient and Persevere** – God's timing is perfect and waiting builds our trust in Him.
  - Isaiah 40:31 (NKJV)
  "But those who wait on the Lord shall renew their strength; they shall mount up with wings like eagles, they shall run and not be weary, they shall walk and not faint."

- **Worship Through the Waiting** – Praising God even in uncertainty strengthens our spirit.
  - Acts 16:25–26 (NKJV)
  "But at midnight Paul and Silas were praying and singing hymns to God, and the prisoners were listening to them. Suddenly there was a great earthquake, so that the foundations of the prison were shaken; and immediately all the doors were opened and everyone's chains were loosed."

HOME SPUN WORD

- Doubt weakens faith, but standing firm in God's promises brings victory.

- Overcome doubt by immersing yourself in God's Word and speaking His truth.

- Trust God's timing, stay patient and worship through every season.

Are you wrestling with doubt today? Refuse to let it steal your breakthrough. Stand on God's Word, declare His promises and hold fast to your faith.

Chapter 8

Live with Boldness and Confidence in God

God has not called us to live timidly, but to walk in boldness and confidence. True faith is accompanied by courageous action, knowing that God is with us every step we take. When we fully understand who we are in Christ, we can step forward in faith, unshaken by fear, doubt or opposition.

The Power of Bold Faith

2 Timothy 1:7 (NKJV)
"For God has not given us a spirit of fear, but of power and of love and of a sound mind."

Many believers struggle with fear, insecurity and hesitation when it comes to walking in their God-given calling. However, boldness comes from a firm foundation in Christ, knowing that we are chosen, equipped and empowered by His Spirit.

Why Boldness Matters

- **Boldness Comes from Knowing Who You Are in Christ**
  – When we understand our identity as children of God, we walk with confidence.
  - Romans 8:15 (NKJV)
    "For you did not receive the spirit of bondage again to fear, but you received the Spirit of adoption by whom we cry out, 'Abba, Father.'"

- **Confidence Grows Through Trusting God's Promises**
  – When we stand on His Word, we gain the strength to move forward.
  - Hebrews 10:35–36 (NKJV)
    "Therefore do not cast away your confidence, which has great reward. For you have need of endurance, so that after you have done the will of God, you may receive the promise."

- **Fear Is Defeated by Faith** – The enemy will try to instil fear, but faith overcomes all fear.
  - ○ Psalm 27:1 (NKJV)
    "The Lord is my light and my salvation; whom shall I fear? The Lord is the strength of my life; of whom shall I be afraid?"

How to Walk in Boldness and Confidence

- **Speak God's Word Over Your Life**
  - ○ Proverbs 18:21
    "Life and death are in the power of the tongue."
- **Take Action Even When You Feel Fear** – Courage isn't the absence of fear; it's choosing to move forward anyway.
  - ○ Joshua 1:9
    "Be strong and of good courage..."
- **Pray with Authority** – Pray with boldness and you will see results.
  - ○ Mark 11:24
    "Whatever things you ask when you pray, believe that you receive them, and you will have them."

Examples of Bold Faith in Scripture

- **David vs. Goliath** – David didn't let fear stop him. He declared victory before the battle even began (1 Samuel 17:45–47).
- **Esther's Courage** – She risked her life to save her people, trusting in God's plan (Esther 4:16).
- **Peter Walking on Water** – He stepped out in faith, trusting Jesus (Matthew 14:28–29).

HOME SPUN WORD

- Bold faith requires confidence in God's promises.

- Fear is conquered by stepping out in faith.

- Speak the Word, take action and pray boldly to live with confidence in God.

Is fear holding you back? Remember, boldness is not a personality trait; it's a spiritual position. When you know who your God is and who you are in Him, you can walk with boldness and confidence into everything He's called you to do.

Chapter 9

Stepping into Divine Opportunities

God is always opening doors of opportunity for you, but it requires faith, obedience and spiritual discernment to step into them. Many times, we miss our God-ordained opportunities because of fear, hesitation or a lack of preparedness.

Revelation 3:8 (NKJV)
"I know your works. See, I have set before you an open door, and no one can shut it; for you have a little strength, have kept My word, and have not denied My name."

Recognising Divine Opportunities

- **God's Timing Is Always Perfect** – Opportunities arise at the right time; we must trust His timing.
  - Ecclesiastes 3:1 (NKJV)
    "To everything there is a season, a time for every purpose under heaven."
- **Opportunities Require Action** – Stepping into God's plan requires faith and obedience.
  - James 2:17 (NKJV)
    "Thus also faith by itself, if it does not have works, is dead."
- **Discernment Is Key** – Not every open door is from God; we must seek His wisdom.
  - Proverbs 3:5–6 (NKJV)
    "Trust in the Lord with all your heart, and lean not on your own understanding; in all your ways acknowledge Him, and He shall direct your paths."

How to Prepare for Divine Opportunities

- **Stay Close to God in Prayer** – Prayer helps us recognise when God is opening a door.
  - Jeremiah 29:12–13 (NKJV)
    "Then you will call upon Me and go and pray to Me, and I will listen to you. And you will seek Me and find Me, when you search for Me with all your heart."

- **Develop Your Gifts and Skills** – God uses our talents to position us for the right opportunities.
  - Proverbs 22:29 (NKJV)
    *"Do you see a man who excels in his work?
    He will stand before kings; he will not stand before
    unknown men."*

- **Be Willing to Step Out in Faith** – Faith is necessary to walk through open doors.
  - Hebrews 11:6 (NKJV)
    *"But without faith it is impossible to please Him,
    for he who comes to God must believe that He is, and
    that He is a rewarder of those who diligently seek Him."*

- **Surround Yourself with Wise Counsel** – Godly mentors and spiritual leaders can confirm His direction.
  - Proverbs 11:14 (NKJV)
    *"Where there is no counsel, the people fall;
    but in the multitude of counsellors there is safety."*

Biblical Examples of Stepping into Divine Opportunities

- **Joseph in Egypt** – Despite trials and setbacks, Joseph remained faithful, and God positioned him to save a nation (Genesis 41:39–41).

- **Esther's Courage** – Esther stepped into her God-ordained purpose to save her people (Esther 4:14).

- **Paul's Missionary Journeys** – Paul followed the leading of the Holy Spirit to spread the Gospel across nations (Acts 16:9–10).

HOME SPUN WORD

- God provides divine opportunities, but we must recognise and act on them.

- Preparation, prayer and discernment are essential for stepping into God's plan.

- Trust that God's timing is perfect and be willing to move when He calls.

Are you positioned for God's open doors? Don't let fear, delay or distraction cause you to miss what He's prepared for you. Stay prayerful, stay ready, and when the door opens, step through in faith.

Chapter 10
Walking in Divine Favour

God's favour is a powerful force that opens doors, creates opportunities and releases blessings beyond what we could achieve on our own. Walking in divine favour means living under God's supernatural grace, where His hand moves on our behalf in ways we could never orchestrate ourselves.

What Is Divine Favour?

Psalm 5:12 (NKJV)
"For You, O Lord, will bless the righteous; with favour You will surround him as with a shield."

God's favour is His unearned, undeserved kindness poured out on our lives. It brings breakthroughs, protection and supernatural blessings that cannot be explained by natural means.

Why Walking in Favour Is Important

- **Favour Opens Doors No Man Can Shut** – God's favour will place you in positions that your qualifications or background alone never could.
  - Revelation 3:8 (NKJV)
    "See, I have set before you an open door, and no one can shut it."
- **Favour Brings Supernatural Increase** – God's favour multiplies what you have and blesses the work of your hands.
  - Genesis 39:21 (NKJV)
    "But the Lord was with Joseph and showed him mercy, and He gave him favour in the sight of the keeper of the prison."
- **Favour Provides Protection** – Divine favour surrounds those who walk with God, shielding them with His supernatural protection.
  - Psalm 91:10–11 (NKJV)
    "No evil shall befall you, nor shall any plague come near

your dwelling; for He shall give His angels charge over you, to keep you in all your ways."

How to Walk in Divine Favour

- **Seek First the Kingdom of God: PUT GOD FIRST –** When we prioritise God's will, He adds blessings to our lives.
  - Matthew 6:33 (NKJV)
    "But seek first the kingdom of God and His righteousness, and all these things shall be added to you."

- **Live a Life of Obedience –** Favour follows those who walk in obedience.
  - Deuteronomy 28:1–2 (NKJV)
    "Now it shall come to pass, if you diligently obey the voice of the Lord your God…that all these blessings shall come upon you and overtake you…"

- **Speak Favour Over Your Life –** Confess and declare God's favour daily.
  - Proverbs 18:21 (NKJV)
    "Death and life are in the power of the tongue, and those who love it will eat its fruit."

- **Stay Humble and Grateful –** Humility attracts God's favour.
  - James 4:6 (NKJV)
    "God resists the proud, but gives grace to the humble."

Biblical Examples of Favour

- **Esther Found Favour with the King –** Her favour led to the deliverance of an entire nation (Esther 2:17).

- **Daniel Was Promoted in Babylon –** His faithfulness and wisdom brought him into favour with kings (Daniel 1:9).

- **Mary, the Mother of Jesus –** She was chosen for a divine purpose because she found favour with God (Luke 1:30).

HOME SPUN WORD

- God's favour brings supernatural opportunities, increase and protection.

- Obedience, humility and faithfulness attract divine favour.

- Favour is not limited; it is available to every believer who walks with God.

You don't have to strive for favour; you receive it by walking closely with the Lord. Speak it, believe it and live in it. Divine favour will surround you like a shield.

Chapter 11

Living in the Overflow of God's Blessings

God's desire is not just to meet our needs, but to bless us abundantly, so that we can become a blessing to others. Living in the overflow means walking in the fullness of His provision, joy and peace.

John 10:10 (NKJV)
"The thief does not come except to steal, and to kill, and to destroy. I have come that they may have life, and that they may have it more abundantly."

What Does It Mean to Live in the Overflow?

- **Experiencing God's Abundance** – God is more than enough for every situation and has more than enough to give away.
  - Philippians 4:19 (NKJV)
    "And my God shall supply all your need according to His riches in glory by Christ Jesus."

- **Being a Channel of Blessing** – When we receive, we are called to pour out and bless others.
  - Luke 6:38 (NKJV)
    "Give, and it will be given to you: good measure, pressed down, shaken together, and running over will be put into your bosom."

- **Walking in Joy and Peace** – Overflow is not just material; it is also spiritual and emotional.
  - Romans 15:13 (NKJV)
    "Now may the God of hope fill you with all joy and peace in believing, that you may abound in hope by the power of the Holy Spirit."

Keys to Living in the Overflow

- **Trust in God's Provision** – He is our ultimate provider.
  - 2 Corinthians 9:8 (NKJV)
    "And God is able to make all grace abound toward you,

that you, always having all sufficiency in all things, may have an abundance for every good work."

- **Be Generous in Giving** – Giving opens the door for greater blessings.
  - o Malachi 3:10 (NKJV)
    "Bring all the tithes into the storehouse... and try Me now in this," says the Lord of hosts, "If I will not open for you the windows of heaven and pour out for you such blessing that there will not be room enough to receive it."

- **Stay Connected to the Source** – Abundance flows from intimacy with God.
  - o John 15:5 (NKJV)
    "I am the vine, you are the branches. He who abides in Me, and I in him, bears much fruit; for without Me you can do nothing."

- **Maintain a Heart of Gratitude** – Thanksgiving unlocks more of God's blessings.
  - o 1 Thessalonians 5:18 (NKJV)
    "In everything give thanks; for this is the will of God in Christ Jesus for you."

Biblical Examples of Overflow

- **The Widow's Oil** – God's provision never ran dry when she obeyed (2 Kings 4:1–7).

- **Feeding the Five Thousand** – Jesus multiplied what was surrendered in faith (Matthew 14:13–21).

- **Peter's Miraculous Catch** – A simple act of obedience led to an abundant harvest (Luke 5:4–7).

HOME SPUN WORD

- God desires for you to live in the overflow of His blessings.
- Generosity, trust and obedience will unlock greater abundance.
- Living in overflow allows you to impact others for His Kingdom.

You were not meant to live in lack; you are meant to live in overflow. Trust God. Give generously. Stay connected to the Source. When you live in the overflow, others will be fed by what spills out of your life.

"*Remember, nobody's perfect.*"
Pastor Nellie Roberts

Chapter 12

Walking in Divine Health and Wholeness

God's will is for us to walk in divine health and wholeness, not just physically, but spiritually and emotionally as well. Jesus paid the price for our healing at the cross, and through faith, we can receive and walk in that healing daily.

Isaiah 53:5 (NKJV)
"But He was wounded for our transgressions,
He was bruised for our iniquities;
the chastisement for our peace was upon Him,
and by His stripes we are healed."

God's Promise of Healing and Wholeness

- **Healing Is Part of Our Redemption** – Jesus took our sickness just as He took our sins on the cross.
  - 1 Peter 2:24 (NKJV)
    "Who Himself bore our sins in His own body on the tree, that we, having died to sins, might live for righteousness – by whose stripes you were healed."

- **Faith Activates Healing** – Throughout Scripture, Jesus often said, "Your faith has made you well."
  - Mark 5:34 (NKJV)
    "And He said to her, 'Daughter, your faith has made you well. Go in peace, and be healed of your affliction.'"

- **Walking in Health Requires Wisdom** – We must take care of our bodies and align our lifestyle with God's wisdom.
  - 1 Corinthians 6:19–20 (NKJV)
    "Or do you not know that your body is the temple of the Holy Spirit who is in you, whom you have from God, and you are not your own?"

How to Walk in Divine Health

- **Declare Healing Daily** – Speak God's promises over your body and health.

- **Live a Healthy Lifestyle** – Eat well, exercise, rest and take care of the temple God has given you.

- **Eliminate Stress and Anxiety** – Worry weakens the body, trust in God's peace and provision.

- **Stay in Prayer and Worship** – The presence of God brings healing to your spirit, soul and body.

HOME SPUN WORD

- Jesus paid for your healing; receive it by faith.

- Faith, wisdom and a godly lifestyle lead to divine health.

- Trust God as your healer in every area of life.

You don't have to live in sickness, fear or anxiety. God's Word declares that healing is yours; by His stripes, you were healed. Step into it. Speak it. Walk in divine health and wholeness every day.

"*People are eternal, so always be kind and respectful.*"
Pastor Nellie Roberts

Walking in Supernatural Peace

Peace is one of the greatest gifts God has given His children. Yet many believers struggle to walk in peace because they allow worry, fear and anxiety to dominate their minds. God's peace is not dependent on circumstances; it is a supernatural state of being that comes from trusting God completely.

I once heard someone say, "Worry is like a rocking chair, you think you're moving, but you're not going anywhere." That's exactly what anxiety does: it steals peace and keeps us stuck.

God's Promise Is Peace – Jesus Is Our Prince of Peace

Philippians 4:6–7 (NKJV)
"Be anxious for nothing, but in everything by prayer and supplication, with thanksgiving, let your requests be made known to God; and the peace of God, which surpasses all understanding, will guard your hearts and minds through Christ Jesus."

God's peace goes beyond human understanding and serves as a divine guard over our hearts and minds, keeping us steady through life's storms.

How to Walk in Supernatural Peace

- **Trust in God Completely** – Peace comes when we surrender control and trust God's plan.
  - Proverbs 3:5–6 (NKJV)
    "Trust in the Lord with all your heart, and lean not on your own understanding; in all your ways acknowledge Him, and He shall direct your paths."
- **Keep Your Mind on Christ** – Focusing on God's Word brings peace.
  - Isaiah 26:3 (NKJV)
    "You will keep him in perfect peace, whose mind is stayed on You, because he trusts in You."

- **Pray About Everything (Talk to God about everything)** – Prayer replaces anxiety with supernatural calm.
  - o 1 Peter 5:7 (NKJV)
    "Casting all your care upon Him, for He cares for you."

- **Guard Your Thoughts and Words** – What we meditate on shapes our peace.
  - o Philippians 4:8 (NKJV)
    "Finally, brethren, whatever things are true,
    whatever things are noble, whatever things are just,
    whatever things are pure, whatever things are lovely,
    whatever things are of good report,
    if there is any virtue and if there is anything praiseworthy
    – meditate on these things."

Biblical Examples of Supernatural Peace

- **Jesus Calming the Storm** – In the middle of chaos, He demonstrated perfect peace and unshakable authority (Mark 4:39–40).

- **Paul and Silas in Prison** – They worshipped despite their chains and peace brought a breakthrough (Acts 16:25–26).

- **Daniel in the Lions' Den** – His unwavering trust in God kept him at peace (Daniel 6:22–23).

HOME SPUN WORD

- God's peace surpasses human understanding.

- Trusting in God, meditating on His Word and praying continually are keys to supernatural peace.

- Peace is not dependent on circumstances; it flows from our relationship with Christ.

No matter what you're facing, God's peace is available to you today. It may not change the situation immediately, but it will guard your heart and mind while God works. Let peace be your position. Let Jesus be your anchor.

Chapter 14

Walking in the Power of the Holy Spirit

The Holy Spirit is a person, not just a force or thing. The Holy Spirit is co-equal with God the Father and Jesus the Son. He is our Helper, our Comforter and our Guide. Walking in His power enables us to live victoriously, fulfil our divine purpose and operate in supernatural strength. Without the Holy Spirit, we strive in our own efforts. But with Him, we walk in authority, wisdom and power.

The Role of the Holy Spirit in Our Lives

- **Empowerment and Boldness for Witnessing**
  - Acts 1:8 (NKJV)
    "But you shall receive power when the Holy Spirit has come upon you; and you shall be witnesses to Me in Jerusalem, and in all Judea and Samaria, and to the end of the earth."

- **The Holy Spirit Gives Us Boldness to Share the Gospel**
  - Acts 4:31 (NKJV)
    "And when they had prayed, the place where they were assembled together was shaken; and they were all filled with the Holy Spirit, and they spoke the word of God with boldness."

- **Guidance and Direction** – He leads us into all truth and helps us make godly decisions.
  - John 16:13 (NKJV)
    "However, when He, the Spirit of truth, has come, He will guide you into all truth..."

- **Supernatural Strength and Comfort** – The Holy Spirit strengthens us in times of weakness.
  - Romans 8:26 (NKJV)
    "Likewise the Spirit also helps in our weaknesses."

- **Gifting and Anointing** – Every believer is given spiritual gifts to fulfil their calling.
  - 1 Corinthians 12:4–11 (NKJV)
    "There are diversities of gifts, but the same Spirit."

How to Walk in the Power of the Holy Spirit

- **Develop a Relationship with the Holy Spirit** – Engage in daily communion through prayer and worship.
  - o 2 Corinthians 13:14 (NKJV)
    "The grace of the Lord Jesus Christ, and the love of God, and the communion of the Holy Spirit be with you all."

- *Yield to His Leading* – Obedience to His promptings allows His power to flow through us.
  - o Galatians 5:16 (NKJV)
    "Walk in the Spirit, and you shall not fulfil the lust of the flesh."

- **Pray in the Spirit** – Praying in the Spirit strengthens our faith and aligns us with God's will.
  - o Jude 1:20 (NKJV)
    "But you, beloved, building yourselves up on your most holy faith, praying in the Holy Spirit..."

- **Operate in Spiritual Gifts** – The gifts of the Spirit are given for the edification of the church.
  - o 1 Corinthians 14:12 (NKJV)
    "Even so you, since you are zealous for spiritual gifts, let it be for the edification of the church that you seek to excel."

HOME SPUN WORD

- The Holy Spirit empowers us for boldness, guidance and supernatural strength.

- Yielding to the Holy Spirit's leading helps us to walk in victory.

- Developing a close relationship with the Holy Spirit unlocks divine wisdom and power.

The Holy Spirit is not distant. He is near and ready to empower you daily. Listen for His voice, follow His lead and let His presence transform your life from the inside out. When you walk with the Holy Spirit, you walk in power.

Chapter 15

Living a Life of Faith and Miracles

Faith is the foundation of the Christian walk. Without faith, it is impossible to please God and through faith, we experience the miraculous power of His promises.

Hebrews 11:6 (NKJV)
"But without faith it is impossible to please Him,
for he who comes to God must believe that He is,
and that He is a rewarder of those who diligently seek Him."

The Power of Faith in Daily Life

- **Faith Unlocks Miracles** – Many of Jesus' miracles were performed in response to someone's faith.
  - Matthew 9:22 (NKJV)
    "But Jesus turned around, and when He saw her He said, 'Be of good cheer, daughter; your faith has made you well.'"

- **Faith Sustains Us in Trials** – Trusting God during hardships produces spiritual strength and endurance.
  - James 1:3–4 (NKJV)
    "Knowing that the testing of your faith produces patience."

- **Faith Enables Us to Walk in the Supernatural** – Peter walked on water because he stepped out in faith.
  - Matthew 14:29 (NKJV)
    "So He said, 'Come.' And when Peter had come down out of the boat, he walked on the water to go to Jesus."

How to Strengthen Your Faith

- **Immerse Yourself in the Word** – Faith comes by hearing and meditating on God's Word (Romans 10:17).

- **Speak Words of Faith** – Life and death are in the power of the tongue (Proverbs 18:21).

- **Step Out in Obedience** – Faith requires action. When we obey, we activate God's promises (James 2:17).

- **Pray with Expectation** – Bold prayers lead to bold results (Mark 11:24).

HOME SPUN WORD

- Faith is essential to experiencing the miraculous.
- Strengthening your faith requires immersing yourself in God's Word, prayer and bold action.
- SPEAK FAITH- FILLED WORDS!
- When you step out in faith, God meets you with His power.

Faith is not a feeling; it's a decision to trust God no matter what.

When you move in faith, you move heaven. Keep walking, keep believing and get ready for the miraculous!

"*Don't live in the past, forgive as Christ forgave you.*"
Pastor Nellie Roberts

Marriage – A Covenant of Faith and Love

Marriage is one of the most sacred covenants established by God. It is designed to reflect His love, unity and commitment to His people, His Bride. A strong, faith-filled marriage is built on the foundation of God's Word, unconditional love and unwavering trust in Him.

God Designed Marriage

Genesis 2:24 (NKJV)
"Therefore a man shall leave his father and mother and be joined to his wife, and they shall become one flesh."

God established marriage as a lifelong union between a man and a woman, built on love, respect and faith. Marriage is not just a contract; it is a covenant that mirrors Christ's relationship with the Church.

Keys to a Strong, Godly Marriage

- **Christ at the Centre** – A marriage built on faith in Christ will withstand every storm.
  - Ecclesiastes 4:12 (NKJV)
    "Though one may be overpowered by another, two can withstand him.
    And a threefold cord is not quickly broken."

- **Love and Respect** – Husbands and wives are called to honour and cherish one another.
  - Ephesians 5:25 (NKJV)
    "Husbands, love your wives, just as Christ also loved the church and gave Himself for her."
  - Ephesians 5:33 (NKJV)
    "Nevertheless let each one of you in particular so love his own wife as himself,
    and let the wife see that she respects her husband."

- **Communication and Forgiveness** – Open, honest communication is vital for a healthy marriage.
  - Colossians 3:13 (NKJV)
    "Bearing with one another, and forgiving one another, if anyone has a complaint against another; even as Christ forgave you, so you also must do."

- **Unity in Purpose** – Marriage is a partnership designed to fulfil God's purposes.
  - Amos 3:3 (NKJV)
    "Can two walk together, unless they are agreed?"

- **Commitment in Every Season** – Marriage requires steadfast love and faithfulness.
  - 1 Corinthians 13:7 (NKJV)
    "[Love] bears all things, believes all things, hopes all things, endures all things."

As I always say, "Murder a thousand times, but divorce never! Make no room for the devil, forgive quickly!" That's a whole marriage seminar in two words!

Challenges in Marriage and How to Overcome Them

- **Financial Struggles** – Trust God as your provider and make wise decisions together.

- **Unresolved Conflicts** – Address issues quickly, with humility and grace.

- **Spiritual Differences** – Pray together and seek God's guidance as one.

- **External Pressures** – Protect your marriage from negative influences and distractions.

HOME SPUN WORD

- Marriage is a covenant, not just a contract.
- God must be at the centre for it to thrive.
- Love, respect and commitment are keys to a lasting marriage.

When two people choose to honour God and each other, marriage becomes a beautiful reflection of heaven on earth. Keep Christ at the centre, keep love at the forefront and keep fighting, together, for what God has joined.

Chapter 17

Who Are You?

I once met a man and asked him his name. Instead of answering, he began listing his many doctoral degrees, the number of churches he had founded and how famous he was. When he finished, I looked at him and asked again, "But who are you?" Sometimes, we get so caught up in our titles, achievements and accolades that we forget God sees beyond all of that. He does not define us **by what we do, but by who we are in Him.**

One of the most important questions we must answer in life is: **Who are you?** Your identity in Christ determines how you live, what you believe about yourself and how you walk in the purpose God has for you.

The enemy will always try to confuse your identity. We see it all over the world today, people are confused about their gender, their identity and even think they're animals. **Why is that?** Because if the devil can steal your identity, he will steal your DESTINY. **But God has already declared who you are!**

Your Identity Is in Christ

Jesus was rejected so that we could be fully accepted by God. He endured shame and suffering so that we could walk in freedom and confidence. Your identity is this: you are a child of God.

Ephesians 1:6 (NKJV)
"To the praise of the glory of His grace, by which He made us accepted in the Beloved."

No matter what rejection you've faced, from family, friends or society, God has already accepted you. Your worth is not determined by others but by the fact that you belong to Him. God is not confused about your identity, and neither should you be. He created you with intention, purpose and clarity.

Genesis 1:27 (NKJV)
"So God created man in His own image; in the image of God He created him; male and female He created them."

God made you who you are with divine precision. In a world filled with confusion, **stand firm in the identity God has given you**. You are fearfully and wonderfully made. There is no mistake in His design.

Psalm 139:14 (NKJV)
"I will praise You, for I am fearfully and wonderfully made; marvellous are Your works, and that my soul knows very well."

You are not a mistake. You were created with **value, purpose and divine intention**.
Your gifts, personality, calling and everything about you were handcrafted by God. He made you fearfully and wonderfully, which means you are unique and intentionally crafted with care.

God Knew You Before You Were Born

Jeremiah 1:5 (NKJV)
"Before I formed you in the womb I knew you;
before you were born I sanctified you;
I ordained you a prophet to the nations."

He knew you before your parents ever did. Before you took your first breath, **God had a plan for your life.**
You are not defined by your past, your mistakes or by what others say about you. **You are defined by who God says you are.**

Who Are You in Christ?

2 Corinthians 5:17 (NKJV)
"Therefore, if anyone is in Christ, he (or she) is a new creation; old things have passed away; behold, all things have become new."

You are not your past. You are not your failures. You are not the labels the world has given you. When you accepted Christ, you stepped into a new identity, one that is redeemed, restored and renewed by His grace.

1. **You Are a Child of God** – Your identity begins with knowing you belong to Him.
   o John 1:12 (NKJV)
   "But as many as received Him, to them He gave the right to become children of God, to those who believe in His name."
2. **You Are Chosen and Loved** – You were handpicked by God for a divine purpose.
   o 1 Peter 2:9 (NKJV)
   "But you are a chosen generation, a royal priesthood, a holy nation, His own special people,
   that you may proclaim the praises of Him who called you out of darkness into His marvellous light."
3. **You Are More Than a Conqueror** – You are not a victim; you are victorious in Christ.
   o Romans 8:37 (NKJV)
   "Yet in all these things we are more than conquerors through Him who loved us."
4. **You Are Redeemed and Forgiven** – Your past does not define you; God's grace does.
   o Ephesians 1:7 (NKJV)
   "In Him we have redemption through His blood, the forgiveness of sins, according to the riches of His grace."

How to Walk in Your True Identity

- **Step into Your New Identity by Faith** – Don't let the past dictate your future; walk confidently in who God says you are (2 Corinthians 5:17).
- **Believe What God Says About You** – Reject the lies of the enemy. Stand on the truth of God's Word (Romans 12:2).

- **Speak Life Over Yourself** – Declare who you are in Christ daily (Proverbs 18:21).
- **Live According to Your Purpose** – Walk boldly into what God has called you to do (Ephesians 2:10).
- **Refuse to Let Circumstances Define You** – Your identity is found in Christ, not in your failures, pain or challenges (2 Corinthians 5:17).

Biblical Examples of Identity in Christ

- **Moses** – Thought he was unqualified, but God called him to be a deliverer (Exodus 3:11–12).
- **Gideon** – Saw himself as weak, but God called him a mighty warrior (Judges 6:12).
- **Paul** – Was once a persecutor, but became a great apostle (Acts 9:15).

HOME SPUN WORD

- You are fearfully and wonderfully made by God.

- God knew you before you were born and has a plan for your life.

- Your identity is found in Christ, not in your circumstances or mistakes.

- Walk boldly in who God says you are, not in the lies of the enemy.

As you embrace your true identity in Christ, you will step into the fullness of His calling and promises for your life. You are chosen, loved and created with purpose, for a purpose. Now go ahead and walk in it!

Chapter 18
Faith Is the Key to the Impossible

As we conclude this journey, one truth remains clear: without faith, it is impossible to please God, and with God, all things are possible. Faith is the foundation of every victory, every breakthrough and every promise fulfilled in our lives.

Hebrews 11:6 (NKJV)
"But without faith it is impossible to please Him, for he who comes to God must believe that He is,
and that He is a rewarder of those who diligently seek Him."

Everything we have explored in this book, from possessing the promises, overcoming doubt, stepping into divine opportunities and living in the overflow, hinges on faith.

Faith is the key that unlocks the impossible and brings God's divine plans into reality.

Faith Turns the Impossible into Reality

- **Faith Moves Mountains** – Jesus said if we have faith as small as a mustard seed, nothing will be impossible (Matthew 17:20).

- **Faith Sustains Us Through Challenges** – Trusting God allows us to endure trials with strength (James 1:2–4).

- **Faith Makes Room for Miracles** – Every miraculous act of Jesus was in response to faith (Mark 5:34).

A Personal Testimony of Faith

In 1979, God spoke to us, Pastor Fred and I, to build a house of prayer for the nations. At the time, it seemed impossible. We had no resources, no blueprint and no clear path forward. But we chose to trust God.

Step by step, with unwavering faith, we obeyed His call, believing that He would provide.

Today, what once seemed unattainable has become a reality. And despite every setback, God has restored our church; it's a place where the next generation is being equipped to touch the nations and the world for Jesus.

This is the power of faith in action. When we trust in God, no obstacle is too great, no vision too big and no dream out of reach.

How to Keep Walking in Faith

- **Believe Beyond What You See** – Faith is trusting God even when the path isn't clear (2 Corinthians 5:7).
- **Step Out with Boldness** – Fear paralyses, but faith activates the impossible (Joshua 1:9).
- **Keep Your Eyes on Jesus** – He is the author and finisher of your faith (Hebrews 12:2).

HOME SPUN WORD

- Faith unlocks the impossible.
- Every promise, breakthrough, and miracle begins with believing God.
- Don't wait for things to look possible, believe, step out and watch God move.

As you move forward in faith, may you possess every promise, overcome every obstacle and walk in the fullness of God's divine plan for your life. Nothing is impossible for those who believe! May this book be a blessing to you, equipping you to live a life of unwavering faith, steadfast trust and victorious purpose, overflowing with the power and presence of Christ Jesus. Amen.

" *Always put God's word first.***"**
Pastor Nellie Roberts

Stay Connected to the Legacy

Scan the QR code to visit the official Dr Fred and Pastor Nellie Legacy Page on YouTube.

There you'll find timeless messages, moments of faith and Spirit-filled teachings that continue to inspire and transform lives. Watch, share, and be part of carrying their legacy forward – one soul, one story, one message at a time – to win the lost at any cost.

www.ingramcontent.com/pod-product-compliance
Lightning Source LLC
Chambersburg PA
CBHW081239020426
42331CB00013B/3229